Better Homes and Gardens®

Your Baby

HEALTHY EATING

Birth–3 Years

BETTER HOMES AND GARDENS® BOOKS

Editor: Gerald M. Knox
Art Director: Ernest Shelton
Managing Editor: David A. Kirchner
Department Head: Sharyl Heiken
Associate Department Head: Elizabeth Woolever
Test Kitchen Director: Sharon Stilwell

President, Book Group: Jeramy Lanigan
Vice President, Retail Marketing: Jamie L. Martin
Vice President, Administrative Services: Rick Rundall

BETTER HOMES AND GARDENS® MAGAZINE
President, Magazine Group: James A. Autry
Editorial Director: Doris Eby
Editorial Services Director: Duane L. Gregg

MEREDITH CORPORATION OFFICERS
Chairman of the Executive Committee: E.T. Meredith III
Chairman of the Board: Robert A. Burnett
President: Jack D. Rehm

YOUR BABY: HEALTHY EATING

Editor: Joyce Trollope
Contributing Editor: Michael P. Scott
Editorial Project Manager: James D. Blume
Graphic Designer: Randall Yontz
Electronic Text Processor: Paula Forest
Contributing Photographers: Kathryn Abbe,
    Bob Ebel Photography

ACKNOWLEDGMENTS

American Academy of Pediatrics, Elk Grove Village, Illinois
American Council on Science and Health, New York City
American Dental Association, Chicago
American Dietetic Association, Chicago
Samuel J. Fomon, M.D., Professor, Department of Pediatrics,
    University of Iowa, Iowa City, Iowa
La Leche League International, Franklin Park, Illinois
Mark Thoman, M.D., Des Moines, Iowa
U.S. Food and Drug Administration, Washington, D.C.

Our seal assures you that every recipe in *Your Baby: Healthy Eating* has been tested in the Better Homes and Gardens® Test Kitchen. This means that each recipe is practical and reliable, and meets our high standards of taste appeal.

CONTENTS

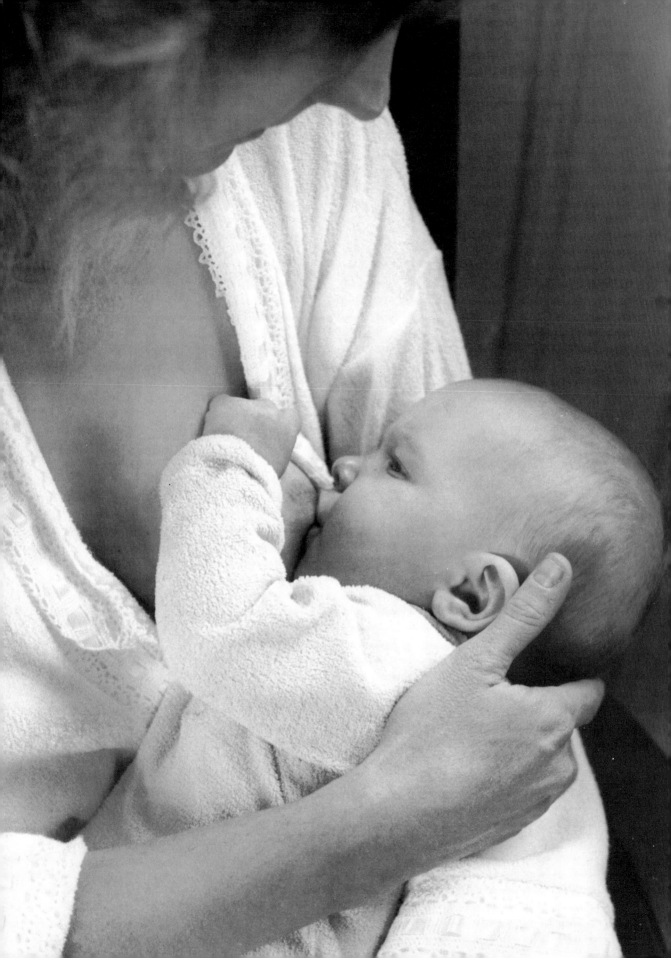

BREAST- OR BOTTLE- FEEDING

Children are nourished in many ways. From the affection lavished on them by adoring relatives, babies grow up knowing the security of love. From the stimulation of their senses come inquisitive minds.

Later, nourished by knowledge from books, teachers, observation of the world, and the endless experiences that make up life itself, a child's intellect develops to its fullest potential.

Such mental and emotional forms of nourishment are truly important, but there's another crucial kind of nourishment found only in the foods your newborn baby will eat.

For it's food that provides energy for all the growing that lies ahead. Contained within a newborn's foods are the calories, vitamins, minerals, fats, proteins, and carbohydrates that will help protect him or her against disease and help build cells, skin, bones, and organs.

Especially for the newborn, nothing could be more true than the old saying, "You are what you eat." But since babies can't choose their menus, the total responsibility for selecting a diet that will ensure a baby's current and future well-being falls on the shoulders of the parents.

BREAST OR BOTTLE— IS ONE BETTER?

Virtually without exception, the best food for babies is their mother's milk. Even the manufacturers of infant formula, who despite their best efforts have yet to come up with an infant formula that *exactly* duplicates breast milk, concede that breast milk is the most appropriate nourishment for newborns.

And although the popularity of breast-feeding comes and goes, these days more mothers are embracing the concept than not. The U.S. Surgeon General now reports that 61 percent of American women plan to breast-feed their babies. Even among mothers who say they plan to return to a job outside the home after their babies are born, half say they plan to breast-feed.

Still, even though the pendulum has once again swung back to favor breast-feeding, many mothers can't or choose not to breast-feed, or feel their activity will be restricted if they do. As a result, they choose bottle-feeding for their babies. And they can make that decision without guilt.

Although such prestigious groups as the American Academy of Pediatrics routinely encourage breast-feeding, they also admit, "Normal growth and development are possible without it."

You only have to look around to see examples of babies who have been formula-fed and grown up healthy. Indeed, you may be one of these bottle-fed babies.

Another reason for choosing formula over breast milk is that the baby's father can take a more active role in feeding the baby when a bottle is used.

The question of whether to breast- or bottle-feed your baby is surrounded by strong and emotional arguments, pro and con. But in the end, the decision is almost always a parental exclusive. Listen to both sides of the debate before making your decision.

Remember, though, that it is your decision. Don't let your feelings and attitudes be swayed too much by the well-meaning opinions of others. If you elect to breast-feed, make the decision based on how you and your baby will be affected. Always keep your options open and retain the right to change your mind if the experience of nursing your baby isn't as successful as you had hoped.

Realize, too, that if you change your mind about bottle-feeding, breast-feeding can be started again days and even weeks after the baby's birth.

HEALTH BENEFITS

Are there definite health benefits to breast-feeding? In many parts of the world, where hygiene, water quality, and refrigeration are not up to American standards, breast-feeding may make the difference between survival and death.

But in the United States, there's no cut-and-dried answer to the question of whether breast-fed babies are healthier. Some studies report fewer health problems among breast-fed babies; others show no differences between breast- and formula-fed babies when other factors are equal.

The health-related advantages usually cited for breast-feeding include a tendency for breast-fed babies to have fewer respiratory and intestinal infections, as well as fewer allergic sensitivities throughout their lives.

THE EMOTIONAL SIDE OF FEEDING

Certainly, a baby's need for food is satisfied by feeding, whether it's at the breast or from a bottle. But there's much, much more to feeding than just food. The very act of feeding your baby, with all the cuddling and rocking that goes along with it, is a crucial source of the warmth, security, and love your baby instinctively needs.

For parents, the nurturing that accompanies feeding, be it by breast or bottle, is an expression of love that helps to cement bonds between them and their babies that will last a lifetime.

AND IF YOU CAN'T OR DON'T BREAST-FEED?

Many couples choose to feed their new babies with bottles so the fathers can be more involved in the process. Other reasons for bottle-feeding may include a mother's career outside the home, extensive travel away from the baby, or, on rare occasions, an inability to breast-feed.

When you choose to bottle-feed your baby, you can do so with the assurance that normal growth and development of your baby are possible without breast-feeding.

In the hospital or birthing center, nurses will introduce your baby to formula-feeding and show you how to give the baby the bottle so you're well prepared when you go home.

Whether you feed your baby by breast or bottle, be sure to lavish as much affection as you can while the baby is feeding. The love you show your child and the emotional bonds you forge are at least as important as the nutrients contained in the milk.

CAN YOU BREAST-FEED YOUR BABY?

The answer is a qualified "yes." An occasional mother may produce insufficient milk to nurse her baby, but these mothers are definitely the exception rather than the rule. Ordinarily, most mothers are able to produce enough milk to meet at least their babies' initial nutritional needs.

Some women may think that, because of their relatively small breast size, they cannot nurse their babies. Rest assured that breast size has nothing to do with the amount of milk produced. Milk production is determined instead by a network of vessels and milk ducts within the breast and the amount of sucking a baby does. Nipples that are flat or turned inward do not automatically rule out breast-feeding either.

Mothers who for one reason or another must take certain medicines (anticancer drugs, thyroid medication) may not be able to nurse, because their medicines could adversely affect their breast-feeding babies. If you must take medicines while you are nursing, *always* check with your—and your baby's—doctor first.

One mistake nursing mothers sometimes make is to supplement the baby's diet of breast milk with water or formula too soon. Such early supplements mean the baby won't take as much breast milk, slowly causing the production of breast milk to diminish and, if repeated frequently, eventually stop altogether.

WILL THERE BE ENOUGH MILK?

The delicate mechanism that controls the mother's production of breast milk ensures that the more milk the baby takes, the more the mother supplies. That rule applies even if you have twins. The normal breast produces between one-and-a-half and two ounces of milk every two to three hours. Each day, a newborn baby requires only about two fluid ounces of milk per pound of body weight. So the amount of milk produced by *both* breasts each day and the typical newborn's need balance out.

New mothers sometimes become concerned when they see breast milk for the first time. Unlike cow's milk, breast milk is not white, thick, or foamy. Instead, breast milk is thin and watery, with a skim-milk bluishness. But appearances aside, this combination of nutrients and consistency is just what a newborn requires. Breast milk is rich enough—about 20 calories per ounce—to supply the 350 calories per day the baby needs.

The best test of breast milk's quality and quantity is how well the baby grows. A baby that appears to be thriving and filling out is probably getting the right amount of nutrients. Don't let the fact that your baby loses some weight right after coming home discourage you from breast-feeding. Most babies lose a little weight then, but they soon start to gain it back—at the rate of about a quarter pound a week.

DAD LENDS A HAND

One nice thing about bottle-fed babies is that they don't complain about which parent feeds them. That makes it easier to share the late-night responsibilities and may ease a working mother's transition back into the workaday world.

Obviously, the father's role in breast-feeding is a different story. But even when a baby is breast-fed, Dad can be an important part of the process.

When Mom goes out alone, Dad can feed the baby a bottle of hand-expressed breast milk. Some fathers of breast-fed babies make it their responsibility to get up at feeding time during the night and bring the baby to the mother.

Advocates of breast-feeding say one of the most important roles a father can play is to provide moral support and companionship while the mother is nursing. And, apart from showing his encouragement, a father also can assume a greater than normal share of the household duties (including caring for other children), so that the mother's time and energy can be focused on nursing and routine baby care.

A NURSING DIET

You'll need to consume about 300 more calories per day while you're nursing your baby than you did when you were pregnant. And if you're under 20 and still growing, you'll require an even greater number of calories.

A nursing mother's diet is slightly different from the one you followed while you were pregnant—you need less protein and more vitamin-rich foods.

Avoid cigarettes and alcohol. Always check with your doctor or pediatrician before taking drugs. Even such common drugs as aspirin and mild laxatives may find their way into breast milk.

And to help milk production, be sure to increase the amount of liquids you drink. In addition to the liquids listed below, you should try to drink a glass of water before and after each feeding.

Here is a daily menu, typical of the meals a nursing mother should eat:

Breakfast
Small glass orange juice
½ cup oatmeal with brown sugar
Full cup milk (some may be used on
    oatmeal)

Lunch
Tuna sandwich made with 2 slices of whole
    wheat bread, ½ cup tuna salad
1 small banana
Full cup milk

Afternoon snack
½ cup peanuts
Full cup milk

Dinner
6 ounces roast beef
½ cup egg noodles
¾ cup cut asparagus
Spinach salad with oil and vinegar
Full cup milk

Evening snack
2 oatmeal-raisin cookies
Full cup milk

Another test of whether your baby is getting enough milk is what can be called the "rule of the diapers." More than six wet diapers each day usually means your baby is getting enough fluid.

STARTING BREAST-FEEDING

A first-time mother's milk will arrive from one to three days after her baby is born, even if the baby is premature. (Mothers who have already had babies may find that their milk arrives a bit earlier.) In the meantime, the baby receives special nourishment from a just-right substitute, colostrum, which is produced by the breasts just before birth (sometimes leaking from the nipples) and remains present in breast milk for about 10 days.

You'll want to put your baby to your breast within hours of giving birth and continue to feed the baby every two or three hours thereafter.

Don't become discouraged if your baby won't nurse or fusses when nursing. There's probably nothing wrong with your milk or your baby. Nursing requires some learning on your baby's part, too. Remember, bottle babies also fuss, cry, spit up, and refuse to eat at times.

If you've never breast-fed before, you may want to get some advice before the baby arrives from the group generally acknowledged to be the breast-feeding experts: La Leche League International. There are local La Leche groups in most communities (check with the obstetrics department of your local hospital). You also can obtain material from physicians' offices or by writing directly to the League's headquarters: P.O. Box 1209, Franklin Park, IL 60131.

At first, you'll probably want to lie down while breast-feeding your baby. The technique is easy to master.

If the baby is nursing from the right breast, lie on your right side and place your arm at the top of or under the baby's head (whichever is more comfortable for you), using your hand and forearm to support the baby. While babies are instinctively proficient at finding the source of their nourishment, you may want to help by holding the nipple between your thumb and forefinger and gently guiding the baby toward it. Babies also move toward the direction of touch. So to get your baby to move toward your breast, stroke the cheek closer to the breast.

Lift the breast from beneath so the nipple—including the brown area surrounding it—is taken into the baby's mouth. Then pull the baby's feet toward your body so his or her nose is unobstructed.

If you want to nurse while sitting up, choose a rocking chair, a low comfortable chair with arms, or the corner of your most comfortable sofa. Sit well back and place a small pillow under your elbow on the feeding side (or double a pillow under the baby so he or she can reach your breast without bending forward). Hold the baby in the crook of your elbow in a semisitting position. Guide the baby toward the nipple with your free hand. When you change breasts, shift the pillows and support to the other side.

When the baby finishes nursing, or when you're ready to switch breasts, gently insert your little finger into the corner of the baby's mouth to release the suction created by nursing. If you just pull the baby away from your breast, you'll likely make your nipple sore. To encourage an uninterested baby to nurse, try stroking his or her mouth or cheeks to stimulate the sucking reflex. Right after they're born, some babies are uninterested in feeding. But their appetites usually pick up by the time the mother's milk arrives. And, as you gain more confidence in your ability to breast-feed, you'll probably produce more milk which your baby will readily consume.

WHEN AND HOW MUCH TO FEED

Babies' eating habits are as different as babies themselves; some are voracious eaters, others are dainty. As far as "how often?" is concerned, one thing is certain: whether they're breast- or bottle-fed, babies need to be fed fairly frequently.

Usually, a newborn wants to be fed from six to eight times a day with two to five hours between feedings. But don't count on a regular 6 a.m., 10 a.m., 2 p.m., 6 p.m., 10 p.m., and 2 a.m. schedule. Your baby may decide he or she

wants to be fed at 6 a.m. and again at 9 a.m. and then not again until 2 p.m. Breast-fed babies usually need to be fed more often than bottle-fed infants. Some breast-fed babies insist on feedings every hour, but, thankfully, they're rare.

The frequent feedings demanded by breast-fed babies may sound tiring or restricting at first. But mothers who have adjusted to breast-feeding say they are unaware of just when, exactly, they feed their babies.

"How much" depends on the baby and how long it takes to satisfy him or her. One of the major goals of infant feeding is to teach the life-long habit of eating in moderation. Right from the first, you should stop feedings just as soon as the baby indicates a willingness to do so.

You may want to begin breast-feeding by placing the baby on each breast for 10 to 15 minutes at a time. Some babies will nurse longer than 15 minutes and some infants will nurse less than 10 minutes.

New mothers sometimes think they've lost their milk when, a week or so after their milk comes in, the feeling of fullness in their breasts subsides and the breasts stop their spontaneous leaking of milk. These signs are actually evidence that your milk supply is adapting to your baby's demand for it.

MAKING BREAST-FEEDING WORK

There's a time and place for everything, except it seems when it comes to breast-feeding. The time is always set by the baby and so, often, is the place. With experience, you'll be able to nurse your baby almost anywhere you choose:

Nevertheless, nursing your baby will probably be more successful if you establish a regular, relaxed routine. Pick a comfortable chair in a restful room and use the time you're nursing your baby to cuddle and talk to him or her. These are precious moments with your infant, so make the most of them.

For your comfort (and the baby's), you'll want to nurse when the baby is ready to eat. If your baby wakes to eat earlier than normal, don't watch the clock waiting for the "scheduled" time to arrive. On the other hand, if your baby tends to oversleep, you may want to get into the habit of rousing the slumbering infant and starting the feeding. Otherwise, your breasts may feel full and sore and milk may begin to leak from them.

WHAT IF YOU WORK OUTSIDE THE HOME?

Many mothers experience no problems breast-feeding their babies *and* continuing their careers outside the home. If you want to resume a workplace career, your ability to juggle work and feedings will probably depend upon how convenient it is for you and your baby to be together during the day.

Some women have careers that allow them to feed their babies at work, perhaps because their employers operate day-care facilities, perhaps because they are able to arrange their work schedules so at-home sitters can bring their babies to them when it's feeding time. Mothers who live near their work may be able to schedule lunches at home for themselves and their babies.

And even when you can't actually be with the baby at feeding time, it's a fairly easy process to keep baby supplied with breast milk. Milk can be hand-expressed (or drawn out with a breast pump) and placed into a relief bottle for use when you're away. Some women hand-express their breast milk while they're at work to maintain their regular milk-production schedules. They then store the milk in refrigerators or chilled vacuum bottles for feeding at a later time.

BREAST-FEEDING AND HOME LIFE

The demands and interruptions that greet you when you return home with your new baby may, at first, seem overwhelming. The readjustment to home and new baby could affect your milk supply if you're not prepared for changes in your routine.

Just keep in mind that the first few days of breast-feeding will require some getting used to. Your baby's appetite may vary widely, causing you, like many other new mothers, to feel inadequate and uncertain about your milk supply.

The thought of being solely responsible for your baby's feedings can create feelings of being tied down. To overcome such feelings, it's important to realize that you're not the first mother to have doubts, and that breast-feeding, once you've settled into it, isn't really that restrictive.

But if you're to be truly successful and rewarded by the experience, your family must help, too. Your milk supply will be enhanced if you are rested and relaxed, rather than tense and fatigued, so enlist help with the household chores from Dad and any other children.

WHEN VISITORS ARE PRESENT

Use your own judgment when deciding whether to nurse your baby in the presence of visitors. The fact of the matter is that nursing is a natural phenomenon.

Nevertheless, you may want to restrict breast-feeding in front of others during the first few weeks because the combination of company and excitement may hold back your milk flow. Remember that guests should not interfere with your baby's feeding schedule; don't delay any feeding more than a few minutes.

Most nursing mothers agree that once a schedule of feeding has been established, it's OK to spend nursing time in the company of friends or relatives. If you have other children, you can feed the baby while keeping an eye on their play activities. Or, this quiet time can be an opportunity for storytelling and some good, old-fashioned motherly listening.

BOTTLE-FEEDING

Even though approximately 60 percent of babies begin their lives feeding at their mothers' breasts, the percentage soon drops off. That makes for a lot of bottle-fed babies, nearly all of whom thrive and grow up as healthy as their breast-fed counterparts. So mothers who decide—for whatever reason—to switch from breast to formula at any point should not feel guilty.

Bottle-fed newborns consume about two ounces of formula at each of six feedings (every

These days, an array of handy equipment—from disposable bottles to convenient ready-to-feed individual servings—makes bottle-feeding easy.

four hours or so) each day. As your baby grows, he or she will consume more and more formula and require fewer and fewer feedings each day to be satisfied.

What makes bottle-feeding especially easy and convenient today are the different brands and forms of formula and equipment on the market. Formulas themselves come in powdered, liquid concentrate, and ready-to-feed forms. And to enhance the feeding of formula, the manufacturers of bottle-feeding equipment have created quite an array of bottles and nipples for you to choose from.

To take advantage of the many forms, sizes, and colors of bottles available, you might consider using one kind of bottle for formula and another for water. The popular disposable bottles eliminate the need to thoroughly scrub the insides of bottles—just zip off a plastic sack from the roll, place it in the holder, and fill it with formula.

The ultimate in bottle convenience is the ready-to-serve, single-serving bottle. Although not as economical, these bottles are great for short day trips in the car to visit friends.

When you're shopping for baby-feeding equipment, you're sure to encounter color-coded nipples. They're designed to help you distinguish among different liquids—for instance, formula, juice, water, and milk—and compensate for their different consistencies. To precisely regulate the delivery of the bottle's contents to your baby, some manufacturers use laser beams to drill holes in the nipples so that water flows at one rate, formula at another. The various size openings in nipples also accommodate the different feeding rates required by children of different ages.

Nipples themselves are made of rubber or silicone to withstand the wear and tear they'll get from your baby's sucking (as well as to stand up to the fats and acids in milk and juice and the repeated washings). Some nipples are designed to approximate the size and shape of a mother's nipple; special orthodontic nipples are said to promote better development of a baby's teeth and mouth structure, although some physicians question these claims.

If you're buying baby-feeding equipment for the first time, rely on the advice of your pediatrician, other mothers, and trial and error to guide you in your selection of just the right formula, bottle, and nipple for you and your baby.

FORMULA PREPARATION

Most commercially prepared formulas come close to duplicating the composition of mother's milk (although none can claim to be as good as the genuine article), and formula manufacturers continue to improve their products as more is learned about infant nutrition. Most formulas use cow's milk as the main source of protein, although for special situations such as allergic reactions to cow's milk, formulas made from other materials (primarily soybeans) also are available.

The three basic types of formula are:
• Powdered formula, which is mixed with water before serving. If your water supply is fluoridated, check with your doctor before feeding your baby a diet consisting mostly of powdered formula. The amount of fluoride in the water used to mix the formula may be more than an infant should consume.

All it takes is a gentle shake onto the inside of your wrist to test the formula's warmth.

A comfy couch makes an ideal spot for relaxing and feeding your baby his or her bottle.

• Liquid concentrates, which also are mixed with water. Concentrates usually make more formula than you'll need for one feeding and the remainder must be refrigerated.

• Ready-to-feed formulas, which cost the most but require no preparation. Just open the can and serve. Unused quantities must be refrigerated after opening.

The elaborate preparations once required to make formula are—for the most part—a thing of the past. Today, preparing formula is as easy as mixing the ingredients for one bottle or an entire day's supply.

Start by washing and rinsing the bottles—preferably in a dishwasher to sterilize them. Boil the bottles if you don't have a dishwasher. Sterilize the nipples in boiling water, then store them in a clean jar until you're ready to use them.

If you use ready-to-feed formula, all you need do is fill the bottle with the right amount, screw on a clean nipple, and feed.

To use liquid concentrate, combine the right amount of concentrate and water in the bottle and feed. For powdered formula, mix the recommended amount with water, shake up the mixture, and feed.

STORAGE TIPS

Often, you'll make more formula than you need right away. If you do, you'll want to take some simple precautions to ensure against the growth of harmful bacteria, which breed rapidly in milk.

Follow the instructions that come with your particular brand of formula, but in general it's best to prepare formula for only one feeding at a time. If you mix more, refrigerate the extra formula after preparation. Formula should be kept no longer than 24 hours in the refrigerator.

Canned formula must always be refrigerated after it is opened. Use aluminum foil or plastic wrap to cover the container.

Throw out any unused formula that remains in the bottle after a feeding—unless you sense or know from experience that your baby will want to eat again within an hour. Between feedings, keep the formula in the refrigerator to prevent growth of bacteria.

CARING FOR AND CLEANING NIPPLES

The nipple on a baby's bottle must be properly cared for to ensure cleanliness and to assure that the right amount of milk is delivered to the baby.

Constant wear from your baby's mouth, the deteriorating effects of milk, and repeated exposure to heat during cleaning contribute to a relatively short life span for nipples.

Nipples must be checked to be sure that their holes are just the right size to allow the baby to feed easily. If the hole is too small, the baby has to work too hard and tires before being satisfied, meaning he or she will want to eat again sooner than scheduled. A hole that's too large lets too much formula (or water or juice) through and the baby may choke or get filled up before the sucking instinct has been satisfied.

To check whether the opening in the nipple is the right size, hold the bottle upside down and shake it. Formula should drip out at about one to three drops per second. A steady stream means the hole is too large.

Even though nipples are relatively inexpensive to replace, you can, if you like, enlarge a constricted opening by sticking a red-hot needle (heated with a match) through the opening from the outside. Slowly enlarge the opening by wiggling the needle; retest the flow.

Wash nipples in the dishwasher or use a small nipple brush and warm, sudsy water. Squeeze the soapy water through the nipple to make sure the opening doesn't become clogged. If formula cakes inside the nipples or if a scum forms, boil the nipples in water for five minutes. Most manufacturers advise against heating nipples in a microwave oven because of possible damage to the rubber or silicone.

CONCERNS ABOUT WATER QUALITY

You'd think that nothing could be more harmless than water. And indeed, America's water supply is now mostly free of the bacterial contaminants our parents or grandparents had to contend with. Today's water, though, presents a whole new set of problems.

For instance, in some parts of the country, fertilizers, insecticides, and weed killers from farm fields and suburban yards have seeped into the underground water that supplies both city water systems and rural wells.

Although many of these chemicals are known to cause cancer and neurological problems, the extent of their effect on humans who drink water contaminated with them is not fully known.

One doctor who is concerned about how children are affected by carcinogens in the water is Dr. Mark Thoman, a pediatrician who is also one of only 120 board-certified clinical toxicologists in the world. He knows both babies and the ins and outs of chemical poisoning. "Generally speaking," Dr. Thoman says, "breast-feeding mothers act as a 'filter' for their baby's milk. The mother can drink the water, absorb the nutrients, filter out the harmful elements, and pass along a 'safe' product to the baby. Water supplements for breast-fed babies are almost never necessary."

Bottle-fed babies are introduced to water from their first feeding—in the form of water used to manufacture the formula itself, or to dilute the concentrated formula you buy.

Dr. Thoman says city water supplies—especially in larger cities—generally can be regarded as safe. If you're concerned—say, as a result of reading local press reports on water quality—call the local health department for advice. If you're still concerned about the quality of your water supply, there are several alternatives you may want to consider.

Bottled water, available at most supermarkets, may be used. U.S. Food and Drug Administration regulations require bottled water to be safe from chemicals.

Parents can add a commercial water filtering system (usually available from companies that sell water softeners) to provide additional protection.

If water is drawn from a well, state health departments sometimes provide an inexpensive analysis of the water's quality.

If you're traveling in this country, you might consider purchasing a small water-purification device with a charcoal filter that can be attached to the water faucet wherever you go.

If you take your baby to a foreign country, don't use water from the tap. Portable filters can be used in a pinch, but you're better off sticking to bottled waters when mixing formula overseas.

Although you might think that boiling water would be an effective way to eliminate harmful chemicals, Dr. Thoman says, "That was probably a good thing to do in the days when bacteria in the water supply were common. Boiling kills the bacteria. But with chemicals, if you boil the water, you're creating more problems. First, you decrease the amount of water through evaporation and increase the level of the toxins. Second, the heat itself will cause the toxins to bind themselves to the water molecules, which will make it more difficult for the baby's body to get rid of them."

Yet another significant water-related hazard to children is lead, which even at low levels can cause serious impairments. Most often, children contract lead poisoning from old paint chips or from lead-glazed pottery, but water that has run through lead plumbing materials sometimes carries traces of lead, too. If you suspect that there is lead in your plumbing, *do not* use hot water to make baby formula, because hot water dissolves lead faster than cold water does. And if you make the formula first thing in the morning, or after the water has stood several hours in the pipes, allow the cold-water tap to run for three to five minutes to rid your plumbing system of water possibly contaminated with lead.

JUICES

For the first four to five months of their lives, babies need only breast milk or formula to help them grow. So when—and how—to introduce your baby to juices is a matter that's dictated not by need, but by the baby's ability to digest foods other than milk or formula.

Sometime between the fourth and sixth months is when you—with your pediatrician's approval—can start to introduce your baby to fruit juices. (At about the same time, your baby will be ready and able to digest his or her first solid food, probably infant cereal. See "Introducing Solid Foods," page 21.)

Dad's involvement in feeding—
especially formula—is important,
too. The time spent with a child
while feeding creates bonds
that will last a lifetime.

DAILY INFANT-FEEDING GUIDE

Foods	0–4 Months
Human milk or iron-fortified formula	5–10 feedings, 16–32 ounces
Cereals, breads	None
Fruit juices	None
Vegetables, fruits	None
Protein foods	None

Source: American Council on Science and Health

Generally, you should avoid starting your baby on juices from citrus fruits (such as oranges) or tomatoes because they can irritate the baby's developing digestive system. Some fruits also can cause allergic reactions, so it's a good idea to start by giving your baby just one fruit juice at a time until you can tell whether the juice agrees with him or her. Also, wait to offer juice combinations until you know that the fruit blend will agree with your baby.

And you'll find out quickly what agrees with your baby and what doesn't. As one pediatrician put it: "Drink it today, wear it tomorrow." If you start a juice and notice later that your baby has developed a redness around the mouth, and by the next day has a bright red bottom, stop the juice or switch to another variety.

Your pediatrician might recommend that you start with a commercially prepared infant version of apple (sometimes pear or apricot) juice that is low in sugar.

One reason babies are given juice is to help satisfy their hunger without adding extra calories to their diets. Ounce for ounce, infant fruit juices have fewer calories than either breast milk or formula. But don't abuse this natural weight-control device. Babies are supposed to gain weight—approximately tripling their birth weight during the first year alone.

Finally, one of the most important things to remember about juices is a "don't." Many parents offer their babies bottles filled with juice (or milk or formula) as they're putting their charges to bed at night or laying them down for a morning or afternoon nap. This practice, according to the American Dental Association (ADA) and pediatricians, can lead to a condition known as "baby-bottle tooth decay."

During sleep, the natural cleansing action of saliva in the mouth tapers off, leaving the sugary juice, milk, formula, or other sweet liquids to accumulate. The ADA says, "The sugars in these liquids are used as an energy source by the bacteria in plaque, the thin almost invisible film of bacteria and by-products that constantly forms on the teeth.

"In the process, the bacteria produce acids that attack tooth enamel. Each time your child drinks a liquid containing sugars, acids attack the child's teeth for at least 20 minutes. After many such attacks, dental caries (tooth decay) can occur."

Because of the serious dental problems that can result when babies take bottles with juices and other sugary solutions to bed with them, some pediatricians recommend feeding juices *only* from a cup.

VITAMINS AND MINERALS

Right from birth, babies need vitamins and minerals to ensure healthy development. A parent's role is to see to it that the baby's daily

4–6 Months	6–8 Months	8–10 Months	10–12 Months
4–7 feedings, 24–40 ounces	3–4 feedings, 24–32 ounces	3–4 feedings, 16–32 ounces	3–4 feedings, 16–24 ounces
Iron-fortified, single-grain infant cereal	All varieties of infant cereal except cereals with fruit or honey Toast, bagel, or crackers	Iron-fortified infant cereals, other plain hot cereals	Iron-fortified, infant or cooked mixed-grain cereals Unsweetened cereals Bread Rice Noodles, spaghetti
Strained single-ingredient infant juice Adult apple juice, vitamin C fortified (2–4 ounces) (Avoid orange juice and tomato juice)	Infant juice Adult apple juice, vitamin C fortified (4 ounces) (Try juice from a cup)	All 100% juices (Orange juice and tomato juice can be introduced)	All 100% juices (Orange juice and tomato juice can be introduced)
None	Fresh or cooked fruits (mashed bananas, applesauce) Strained fruits or vegetables (1 jar or ½ cup)	Peeled, soft fruit slices or wedges (bananas, peaches, pears, oranges)	All fresh fruits, peeled and seeded Canned fruits or vegetables packed in water
None	Plain yogurt	Lean meat, chicken, and fish (strained, chopped, or small tender pieces), whole egg, cheese, egg yolk, yogurt, mild cheese, cooked dried beans	Small tender pieces of meat, fish, or chicken Yogurt, cooked dried beans

requirement for a dozen or more essential vitamins and minerals is met.

The most recent statement of the American Academy of Pediatrics on vitamins says, "Normal, healthy children receiving a normal diet do not need vitamin supplementation over and above the recommended dietary allowances."

Sometimes a baby may, for many reasons, develop vitamin or mineral deficiencies that can be corrected with supplements. Talk to your pediatrician about any aspects of your baby's family medical history that might raise concerns. If your baby is born prematurely or underweight, the doctor may supplement his or her diet with additional vitamins or minerals.

Seeing to it that a baby's vitamin and mineral requirements are met is relatively easy thanks to considerable study by pediatric researchers over the past 40 years and strict government regulations governing the labeling of baby foods. The nutritional content of infant formulas is clearly marked on the package or can, in terms of both quantity and percentage of the recommended daily allowances.

Breast-fed babies whose mothers eat a well-balanced diet generally do not need additional vitamin or mineral supplements, but the Academy of Pediatrics notes that some breast-fed infants may need to have their diets supplemented with vitamin D and fluoride.

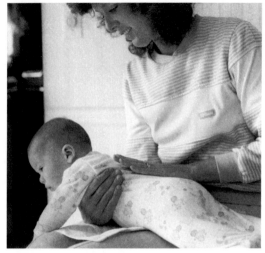

Just a few gentle pats on your baby's back will help expel air swallowed while feeding.

Make sure baby's head is turned to one side. Just getting into position may help your baby burp.

Vitamin D prevents a disease called rickets. This essential vitamin is present in foods and also is produced by the body during exposure to sunlight. Fluoride is well known for its ability to protect against tooth decay. The most accessible source of fluoride is a community's treated water supply. Your doctor may recommend a fluoride supplement for your baby, whether he or she is breast-fed or not. Fluoride in water used for a breast-fed baby's supplemental bottles (after the age of four to six months) and in cooking will provide adequate amounts of this mineral.

Some vitamins are given to newborns as a matter of course. Most babies begin life with a shot of vitamin K, which helps their blood clot and prevents hemorrhaging.

Perhaps the most common nutritional deficiency is iron. Babies' iron needs are high because their blood supplies are growing right along with the rest of them. Most infant formulas produced by reputable manufacturers contain the appropriate amount of iron.

Some formulas are fortified with additional iron. But, because iron is sometimes an irritant to the baby's digestive tract, and excessive amounts can cause colic, you'll want to check with your pediatrician before supplementing your infant's diet with iron.

TIME FOR A PAT ON THE BACK

With all the breast milk or formula your baby is taking in, he or she will also be swallowing air, and that may cause some minor discomfort. But there's an easy solution to the problem: burping.

Burping is nearly always a required part of the feeding routine, although correctly positioned breast-fed babies and bottle-fed babies (those fed in a more or less upright position) may have less discomfort because the air can escape from their tummies almost as soon as it's swallowed.

There are several ways to get rid of accumulated air in the baby's stomach. You'll probably discover that one way of burping works best for you and your baby. One of the most popular methods is to hold the baby upright with his or her head over your shoulder (don't forget to place a towel between you and baby, just in case more than air escapes). This vertical position gives the air in the stomach a straight shot at escape.

Once the baby is resting comfortably over your shoulder, pat or rub the back gently. You can judge your success at bringing up burps just by listening for that reassuring sound of air escaping—often in a resounding BURP!

Another tried-and-true method is to put the baby on his or her stomach on your lap or in the crib. Then, making sure the baby's head is turned to one side or the other to allow air and, occasionally, milk or formula to escape unimpeded, gently rub or pat the baby's back until he or she burps.

You may find that holding the baby in a semisitting position, leaning slightly forward, head and back propped with your hands, is an equally successful position for burping.

And many times, just the exertion of moving the baby into burping position will be enough to expel the trapped air.

Most babies will burp two or three times during and after nursing, but don't worry if yours doesn't burp according to schedule. You can continue with feeding or put the baby to bed on his or her stomach, with the head turned to one side to allow any milk or formula to escape without clogging the mouth or nose.

WHEN BURPS TURN UP MORE THAN JUST AIR

Many times a burp causes the baby to spit up some of the milk or formula he or she has just eaten. Don't worry. As long as it's just a few trickles of milk and not repeated sessions of vomiting with force (projectile vomiting), there's no cause for alarm.

Some babies tend to spit up a lot, others seldom do. There are many reasons babies spit up, including simply eating too much or swallowing too much air during feeding.

If your baby is a persistent spitter, try burping him or her longer and more often. Or, leave the baby a little longer in an inclined infant seat.

If spitting up continues, despite your best efforts at bringing up burps, the explanation may be something more than just too much fluid and swallowed air. For instance, the baby's muscles controlling the passage of milk between esophagus and stomach may not be fully matured. In such cases, the amount of spitting up will lessen as the baby grows older.

Vomiting with force should always be reported to your physician if it occurs after several feedings. Repeated vomiting may dehydrate a baby and might be a sign of illness.

WEANING FROM BREAST-FEEDING

There is no hard-and-fast rule about when to wean an infant from the breast.

Some babies continue to receive part of their daily milk requirement from their mothers well into their second year.

As a general rule, the decision to wean a baby is made with both the baby's nutritional needs and the mother's schedule in mind. Usually by the time babies are between four and six months old, they have started to receive an increasing percentage of their daily nutritional requirements from foods other than breast milk or formula. So, many nursing mothers begin the process of weaning at this time.

Another consideration involves mothers who work outside the home. A return to the work force naturally restricts the number of breast feedings and thus may signal an opportune time to begin weaning.

No matter when you decide to wean your baby, you should plan to do it gradually, for your sake and the baby's. You'll want to consult with your doctor about the proper way to replace breast milk during the weaning period so that your baby receives adequate nutrition.

Although it's possible to wean a baby in a week's time, it probably would be less traumatic for both of you to drop one daily feeding at a time over a period of two to four weeks.

If your baby starts to show a lack of interest in a particular feeding, you might try eliminating that feeding the next day. Many mothers find the noontime feeding the easiest to omit. Some mothers then prefer to eliminate the morning feeding; still others prefer to eliminate the nighttime feeding. Remember, there is no correct schedule for weaning, so the choice will be up to you and your baby.

If weaning occurs at around four to six months, you'll want to replace the breast milk with a bottle of formula. If weaning occurs later, you may simply switch from the breast to a cup.

Because the breasts naturally adjust their production of milk to meet demand, a gradual tapering off of breast-feeding will cause the least discomfort. If for some reason you must stop breast-feeding abruptly, you can hand-express milk until milk production stops.

INTRODUCING SOLID FOODS

By the time your baby is four to six months old, he or she has changed so much and so quickly that you almost have to look at the pictures you took last week to remember what he or she was like "way back when." But then, that's what healthy babies are supposed to do—grow and change.

Among these changes, although admittedly difficult to see, is the development of the muscles, organs, and senses necessary to allow your baby to recognize a spoon, sense the taste of solid foods, and coordinate the work of the tongue and mouth to swallow and then digest these foods.

Unpack the bibs. Your baby, with your help, is about to make his or her first attempts to eat solid foods. Count on things being messy for a while until the technique of eating is completely mastered. And plan on being impressed—and sometimes a little frustrated—with your youngster's growing ability to make decisions about what is or is not going to go into his or her mouth.

Like many things about raising a child, there's no magic formula for timing a baby's shift from a strictly liquid diet of formula or breast milk to a diet made up more and more of solid foods.

Not all that long ago, babies were fed breast milk exclusively until they were about a year old. In the 1920s, pediatricians began recommending that solid foods be started at an earlier age. Today's advice, based on scientific observation plus a good deal of practical experience, is to introduce solid foods sometime between four and six months of age.

If your baby's first tooth has arrived, and he or she is grabbing at food and trying to eat it, offer him or her some cereal. But if the baby repeatedly pushes or tongues this new food out of his or her mouth, wait a week or so before offering cereal again.

Other gauges of a baby's readiness for solid foods include weight (some authorities believe that solid foods can be introduced when a baby's birth weight has doubled) and motor development. Babies who are ready to eat solid foods often are able to sit with support, have good control of their head and neck muscles, and lean forward and open their mouths as though they're anticipating food.

There's no reason to hurry an infant's introduction to solid foods. Some evidence even suggests that one reasonable (although as yet unproven) way to avoid obesity later in life is to delay the offering of solid foods.

GETTING STARTED

Cereal often is the first solid food a baby eats. It's easy to fix and can be watered down to a thin consistency so the transition from breast milk or formula is not so obvious.

Babies, just like their parents, are sometimes bothered by certain foods. Your doctor or pediatrician will likely recommend that you introduce one food at a time, waiting until you see how that food agrees with your baby before adding something else to the diet.

After cereal, the foods you'll introduce may come in this order: fruits, vegetables, meats, and, with the doctor's permission, egg yolks. There's nothing hard and fast about the order in which foods should be introduced, and babies are quick to show their parents which ones they like and don't like. So feel free to do some experimenting with which foods you introduce first.

When your baby is ready for cereal, check the store for a variety of precooked, dehydrated rice, oatmeal, barley, wheat, and mixed cereals fortified with iron. You also can prepare your own baby cereal from whole grains, although you'll lose the additional vitamin fortification offered in the packaged cereals.

Of all the grains, rice is one of the least likely to cause digestive problems or allergic reactions. If your family has a history of allergies to foods, you may want to avoid using wheat or mixed-grain cereals until sometime after the baby's first birthday. Be sure that the baby's doctor knows about any food allergies in both parents' families.

One or two teaspoons of cereal is enough for the first feedings. Follow the directions on the package or simply place the cereal in a clean dish and wet it with warm formula, breast milk, or water. (Later, when the baby is about six months old or so, you can begin to mix cereal with cow's milk.) Stir the cereal until it's well mixed and is almost liquid. Some babies like a very thin cereal, others prefer their cereal thicker.

Some parents attempt to mix cereal thin enough to feed it through a bottle, using a nipple with an enlarged opening. Although it's a less messy way of feeding cereal, this technique is discouraged by pediatricians who believe there's no need to feed a baby foods he or she isn't physically able to eat. This method also may encourage a baby to develop a habit of eating even when he or she is not hungry. Besides not being recommended, this technique also takes some of the fun out of teaching a baby to eat with a spoon.

Start feeding your baby his or her cereal with a small spoon—an iced-tea spoon, for instance, or a specially created baby spoon. With the baby nestled securely in your arm, or in an infant seat, touch the half-filled spoon to the baby's lips. Just the touch of the spoon should be enough to cause the baby's lips to part so you can insert the spoon and cereal.

The baby's upper lip, gums, and tongue will guide the food into the mouth. Be prepared for a mess. You'll want the baby to wear a bib. You may want to wear washable clothes, too, because those first few tastes of food will be a strange experience for your youngster. There's a good chance that your baby's tongue will push this new and "foreign" material right back out. Plan on using the spoon to scrape the food off the baby's chin or bib and trying again.

One of the tricks your baby will be likely to play as he or she learns to eat solid foods is: "Let's see how much food I can blow out (or spit out) on Daddy or Mommy."

When you first start feeding solid foods, give them to your baby only once or twice a day according to your doctor's advice and your baby's appetite.

The actual timing of when to feed cereals is mostly up to you and the baby. Some parents prefer to start with a morning feeding, others prefer to save the fuss and muss until later in the day. You should always first feed the baby just enough milk or formula to take the edge off his or her hunger. Otherwise, the baby may be too hungry to consider new and unfamiliar foods. Conversely, a baby *too* full of milk won't want to try new foods either. Later, the order can be switched so the baby doesn't fill up on milk or formula and ignore the solid foods.

When babies are full, the more cooperative ones simply turn their heads away from bottle, breast, or spoon. But some babies let you know they've had enough by determinedly locking their mouths shut or by taking a bite and waiting till you're looking away before spitting out the food. The point is, when your baby's full, stop feeding.

INTRODUCING DAIRY PRODUCTS

Sometime around the sixth month—but again, there's no precise time—you can start to introduce your baby to dairy products. This is a controversial area of infant nutrition, so before feeding your baby milk from the carton in your refrigerator, check with your baby's doctor for advice. Here are some of the concerns about dairy products you might want to discuss:

• Allergies. Milk is a common cause of allergic reactions. If the baby has been formula-fed, such reactions probably will have been spotted earlier, but occasionally, allergic reactions do not occur until the child first drinks dairy milk. In such cases, a nonallergenic milk substitute, or perhaps goat's milk, should be prescribed.

• Fat. Concerned parents sometimes are eager to switch from formula or breast milk (which are relatively higher in fat content) to low-fat or nonfat cow's milk because of their concerns about obesity. Even though their intentions may be good, these parents, according to the American Academy of Pediatrics, may be doing more harm than good. "It appears that society's obsession with being slim and trim and its fear of heart disease has resulted in another disease—poor growth and delayed development in infancy." Babies need appropriate amounts of fat to ensure the proper development of their

SCHEDULE FOR SOLID FOODS

This chart shows the order in which baby foods are usually, but not necessarily, introduced. The ages listed for when foods should be offered are approximate and will, no doubt, vary from baby to baby. Your baby's doctor is your best source for advice on when and how often a particular food is appropriate.

Formula or breast milk should be used when mixing cereals.

AGE	FOOD	FREQUENCY
4 to 6 months	Precooked baby cereal	Twice a day
	Baby juices	Between meals
5 to 6 months	Strained single fruits	Twice a day
6 to 7 months	Strained vegetables	Once a day
7 to 8 months	Strained meats	Once a day
	Plain yogurt	Once a day
	Baby juices	Between meals
8 to 9 months	Egg yolk, strained	Once a day

Source: *FDA Consumer,* September 1985

brains and nervous systems, for energy, and to make sure that certain fat-soluble vitamins are able to do their work. Some doctors believe that the best compromise between too much and too little fat in milk is 2 percent milk.

Until your baby is about one year old, you should limit milk consumption to about a pint (16 ounces) a day.

24

Your baby's tableware will include feeding dishes, cups, and eating utensils, both for you to feed your baby with and for your toddler to feed himself or herself with. When selecting your baby's tableware, make sure it's strong enough to stand up to the repeated spills from high chair to floor. Don't forget to include an ample supply of bibs. They'll get plenty of use.

• Anemia. Cow's milk is low in iron, and the little it does have is not easily used by human babies. An infant whose diet contains too much cow's milk may develop a condition known as iron-deficiency anemia. Because *too much* iron in the diet can irritate the baby's digestive system, check with your doctor before supplementing your baby's diet with iron.

As with other new foods, introduce dairy milk slowly, observing how your baby reacts.

Cultured dairy products—yogurt or cottage cheese, for instance—are a good way to start.

They're often more palatable and give your baby something on which to try out his or her newly acquired teeth.

Regardless of when your baby starts drinking cow's milk, you can count on a change in the baby's bowel habits. Usually the result will be firmer stools, because cow's milk contains less sugar and fewer carbohydrates than formula.

You may be able to soften the baby's stools by simultaneously introducing more fruit into his or her diet. Prunes, peaches, or apricots usually work well.

ADDING MORE FOODS TO THE BABY'S DIET

For the first six months, milk is the most important food in a baby's life. From six to 12 months, milk and other foods are equally important. And, after 12 months, other foods become more important than milk to the child's development.

What this means, in practical terms for parents, is best expressed in a report on baby foods prepared by the American Council on Science and Health: "After four to six months, solid foods should be added to supplement, but not replace, formula or milk, and their portions gradually increased. Choose commercially prepared or homemade foods that are appropriate for the child's chewing and swallowing abilities. Your ultimate goal is to offer your child a reasonable variety of foods from all four food groups" (meat, fish, poultry, eggs, and beans; dairy products; fruits and vegetables, including potatoes; and breads, cereal grains, rice, and noodles).

"Infant diets should change gradually from all-liquid to part-liquid and part-strained, single-ingredient baby foods. After the single-ingredient foods are accepted, mixed-ingredient foods can be introduced. Textured foods follow, before the introduction of family foods completes the transition to an adult diet. By one year of age, most infants can handle a great diversity of foods. This gradual introduction to a variety of food helps promote good eating habits and contributes to a balanced diet."

You'll want to introduce foods one at a time so you can learn whether the particular food agrees with your baby.

If you've just added a cereal, fruit, or vegetable to your baby's diet, and you suddenly notice diarrhea, constipation, skin rashes, or any other changes in his or her condition, then you won't have any trouble identifying which food caused the problem.

Most of the time, the first foods to be introduced after cereal are fruits. Bananas are a good way to start because they can be prepared easily by mashing up a teaspoon or so in formula or milk. Applesauce, strained pears, and strained peaches usually follow, but you can vary the order according to your (and your baby's) preferences. Citrus fruits such as oranges (and

FOODS THAT MAY CAUSE PROBLEMS

Throughout the first few years of a child's life, certain foods may be upsetting as a result of allergies or an immature digestive system. Here's a list of foods that pediatricians have found may cause troubles when babies first encounter them.

FREQUENTLY CAUSE PROBLEMS

Berries	Corn	Nuts, oils,
Buckwheat	Cow's milk	extracts
Caffeine	Dairy	Peanut
Chocolate	products	butter
Citrus fruits	(all)	Pork
and juices	Egg whites	Wheat
Coconut	Fish (all)	Yeast
Cola drinks		

SOMETIMES CAUSE PROBLEMS

Bananas	Garlic	Potatoes
Beef	Melons	(white)
Celery	Mushrooms	Prunes
Cherries	Onions	Spices
Chicken	Peaches	Spinach
Coloring	Plums	Tomato
agents		products
Cottonseed		Vitamins
oil		

SELDOM CAUSE PROBLEMS

Apples	Ginger ale,	Lamb
Apricots and	noncola	Lettuce
apricot	carbonated	Oats
juice	drinks	Pears and
Bacon	Grapes and	pear juice
Barley	grape juice	Pineapple
Beets	Honey (not	and
Carrots	recom-	pineapple
Cranberries	mended at	juice
and	all for	Raisins
cranberry	children	
juice	under age	
	one)	

What your baby eats will be partly determined by the number of teeth in his or her mouth. Solid foods should be introduced about the time teeth emerge from both jaws.

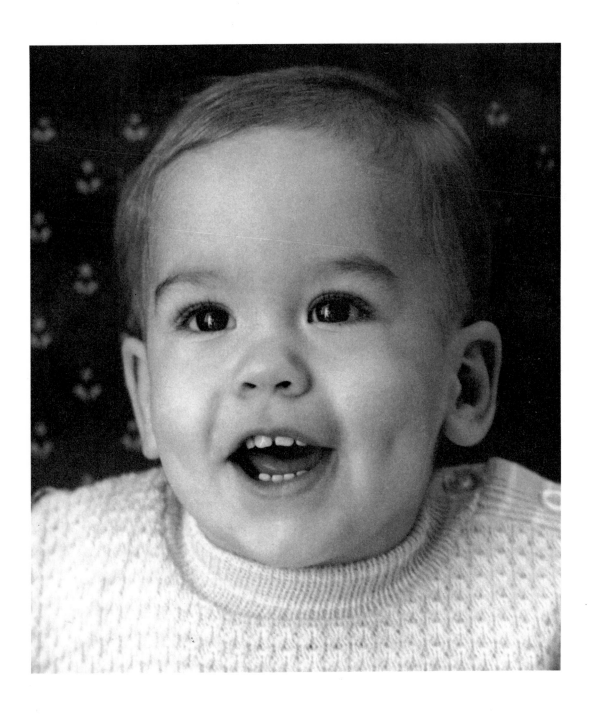

GOOD NUTRITION AT A DAY-CARE CENTER

Today in the United States, about half of working mothers whose children are under age five use some kind of large-group day-care facility. If you fall in that particular category, you're probably wondering what you can do to make sure your baby's nutritional needs are met while he or she is being cared for in your absence.

The American Academy of Pediatrics suggests that your first step be to spend some time talking with the operators of the facility to determine their attitudes, expectations, and competence.

A good facility makes appropriate foods available to children of all ages, but does not use food to reward or punish them. Children should be encouraged but not forced to eat.

Many facilities have a dietitian on staff or on call to prepare a varied menu consisting of selections from all food groups. You should ask to see the facility's meal plan.

Children who remain in a day-care facility for nine or more hours each day should be served at least two meals and two snacks.

If your baby is under 18 months old, you should be allowed to provide formula or hand-expressed breast milk. You also should be able to supply the foods you want your child to eat, along with feeding schedules.

A well-run day-care facility will not prop bottles in babies' mouths and leave them unattended while feeding.

Areas should be specially designated for eating only and the facility should enforce strict hand-washing routines (for children and staff), especially after they've used the toilet, changed diapers, or blown their noses, before they've brushed their teeth, and before and after they've eaten.

If someone cares for your child in your home while you're at work, you should prepare complete and detailed instructions spelling out your expectations for the baby's diet while you're away.

orange juice) are usually one of the last fruits to be introduced, sometime between eight months and one year.

After feeding cereals and fruits for two to four weeks, you can start vegetables (a chief source of carbohydrates). At first, vegetables should be served separately from other foods. Follow the same procedure you used with fruits and cereals: one vegetable at a time until you can see how it agrees with your baby.

Start by serving strained, mild-flavored vegetables. Yellow vegetables such as squash or sweet potatoes are good choices.

Then progress to carrots, beans, and peas; beets and spinach should be the last to be introduced. From the colorful vegetables you're adding to the baby's diet come vitamins and minerals—and often a change in the consistency and color of bowel movements.

Don't worry if your baby does not like some vegetables. And don't, because of your own personal tastes, try to push or withhold certain vegetables. Just try your best to acquaint your baby with a variety of vegetables.

Strained meats come next, usually a month after you've started serving vegetables. Meats are important because, as babies drink less and less milk, they need a new source of protein, iron, and vitamins.

Meat juices, too, play an especially important role in helping the baby's body absorb other forms of iron in the diet.

The most popular meats are beef and chicken, followed by lamb. It is possible to provide a baby with adequate protein from vegetable sources alone, but you'll want to check

WHAT TO DO IF YOUR CHILD CHOKES

The American Academy of Pediatrics, the American Heart Association, and the American Red Cross recommend the following first-aid procedures for choking infants under age one:

Place the infant facedown on your forearm with the head lower than the body. Brace your forearm against your thigh for additional support. Next, with the heel of your hand, rapidly administer four rhythmic back blows high between the baby's shoulder blades. The photo at *right* demonstrates the correct position.

If the object that's causing the choking isn't expelled, or if breathing doesn't start, place the baby on his or her back on a firm surface and deliver four rapid chest thrusts (similar to the compressions used when administering cardiopulmonary resuscitation [CPR]) over the sternum (breastbone) using two fingers. If breathing still does not start, open the mouth with your thumb over the baby's tongue and your fingers wrapped around the baby's lower jaw. If you can see the object causing the choking, remove it with a sweeping motion of your finger.

If these emergency measures fail, get the baby to a medical facility immediately.

For a choking child older than age one:

Place the child on his or her back and kneel next to him or her. Place the heel of one hand on the middle of the child's abdomen between the rib cage and the navel and apply a series of six to 10 rapid inward and upward abdominal thrusts until the object causing the

choking is expelled. This is one way to perform a procedure commonly called the Heimlich maneuver. A two-handed version of the maneuver is used for older and larger children (and adults) while they're sitting, standing, or lying down.

If these attempts do not propel the object from the child's airway, open his or her mouth using the technique described for infants. If you can see the object that's causing the choking, sweep it out of the mouth with your finger.

If the child still does not start breathing, call for emergency help and attempt mouth-to-mouth resuscitation or mouth-to-mouth and mouth-to-nose breathing, then repeat the abdominal thrusts.

Parents, grandparents, and siblings should learn these techniques, the Heimlich maneuver (to treat choking in a child over age one and in adults), and cardiopulmonary resuscitation. Check with your local hospital, Red Cross, or Heart Association for more information.

with your doctor or pediatrician to ensure that the vegetarian diet you've chosen for your baby isn't deficient in vitamins and minerals.

STORE-BOUGHT OR HOMEMADE

The American Council on Science and Health says commercially prepared baby foods "are a wholesome addition to a child's diet. Large manufacturers have at their disposal sophisticated methods of preparation, sterilization, and quality control to assure safety and nutritional adequacy. According to taste tests, they are just as good as homemade products, but of course your baby is the final judge."

Certainly, the sometimes mind-boggling array of little glass jars and packages on display at the grocery store should assure you that with a little imagination and some cooperation, your baby will never lack variety in his or her diet.

Year-round access to seasonal foods makes commercially prepared baby foods appealing to parents who are interested in providing their babies with well-balanced diets. And the federal government—through the Food and Drug Administration and the U.S. Department of Agriculture—closely regulates the labeling of baby foods and thus their quality.

The labels on infant foods (for babies under one year), in fact, are more complete than those found on many adult foods. They must include a list of each ingredient by name (including spices, flavorings, and colorings) and an explanation of the plant or animal source of an ingredient (palm oil rather than just vegetable oil). Most manufacturers also provide listings of the amounts (or percentages of the recommended daily allowances—U.S. RDAs) of calories, protein, carbohydrates, fats, sodium, vitamins, and minerals found in their foods.

Manufacturers—under pressure from parents and consumer groups—have made an effort in recent years to eliminate additives from baby foods and reduce their salt and sugar content. In the past, flavorings often were added to baby foods to satisfy the parents' taste buds and not the baby's.

For control over the ingredients in your baby's diet, though, you can't beat homemade foods. Making your own baby food also allows you to take full advantage of fresh produce.

EQUIPMENT FOR MAKING BABY FOOD

With nothing more complicated than a fork you can convert a banana or cooked egg yolk into baby food by mashing it with some milk, formula, or fruit juice. A blender or food processor makes simple work of converting meats and vegetables into baby food. And an ice-cube tray is a convenient device for freezing small, individual servings of your homemade baby foods.

A saucepan with a steamer basket or a microwave oven allows you to cook vegetables while retaining many valuable nutrients. Boiling vegetables reduces their nutrient content, so if you boil the vegetables, be sure to use a minimal amount of water and to reserve the water for use when pureeing the foods (see pages 40–42).

Although some store-bought foods would be difficult to duplicate in your kitchen (precooked, dehydrated, fortified cereal, for instance), you can easily convert foods you're feeding the rest of your family into nutritious meals for your baby.

Simply set aside some of the vegetables you're preparing before you add spices and seasonings (especially salt) and puree the baby's portion in the blender or food processor.

When you're converting adult foods into infant foods, cook the foods until very tender and remember to remove all stringy material and chunks from the food to prevent choking. Use fresh fruits and vegetables whenever possible to avoid the preservatives and seasonings that are sometimes present in canned or frozen foods. (See page 39 for a cautionary note.)

Serve meat and vegetables separately at first, but after the baby has become accustomed to meat, you can mix it with vegetables to form a stew. Later (usually after 12 months of age when your baby's body is better able to digest starchy materials), you can add noodles or spaghetti to the pureed meat.

STARTING TABLE FOODS

One of the first, and most obvious, milestones in your child's life is the transition from baby foods to table foods. At about age one, most youngsters start to eat foods that are, in many respects, the same as the ones they'll be eating for the rest of their lives.

Before making the switch, your toddler's ability to grasp, taste, chew, swallow, and digest adult foods must have reached the right stage of development.

The American Academy of Pediatrics says this phase of infant nutrition is a "modified adult period, during which the majority of the nutrients come from the foods available from the table."

Unlike many of life's other milestones (first day of school, high school graduation, marriage), this transition is gradual and seldom emotional, except for a few exasperated sighs as your toddler exercises his or her pitching arm, lobbing a few fast meatballs at the family cat.

But, milestone or not, just because your child learns to feed himself or herself doesn't mean you can stop being concerned about good nutrition. A lot of growing lies ahead, and for it to successfully occur, your youngster must continue to eat well.

The transition from baby foods to table foods naturally occurs at a time when your baby's appetite for breast milk or formula is waning. After months of voracious drinking, your baby's desire for milk probably peaked somewhere around the seventh or eighth month.

One reason for this drop in milk consumption is your baby's slowing growth rate. During the first three to four months, your baby probably doubled his or her birth weight. But by the time a year rolls around, your baby will only be about three times his or her birth weight.

A one-year-old's main source of protein is meat; vegetables and fruits supply carbohydrates, sugars, and minerals. A pint of milk each day is probably sufficient, with some of it coming from other sources—mild cheeses and yogurt, for instance. You may find, too, that your baby no

SPECIAL FEEDING TIPS

• Allergies. The foods listed in the tip, "Foods That May Cause Problems," page 25, sometimes cause allergic reactions. Babies often outgrow their allergies, usually by the age of two. If there's an allergy to milk, nondairy substitutes can be used. For other foods, usually the best advice is to avoid the problem food.

• Colic. Babies who cry persistently for no apparent reason are sometimes referred to as colicky. At one time, colic was assumed to result from intestinal cramping, but today, most physicians believe that colic is simply a result of the baby's still immature nervous system. Most babies grow out of this stage by three months of age no matter what treatment is provided.

Sometimes a particular brand of formula causes the colic. For those cases, switching to a formula with a different base—soybeans, for instance—may be the solution. In any event, you'll want to check with the baby's doctor to make sure that any persistent crying is not the result of a more serious problem.

• Dangerous foods. Do not give a baby under a year old foods that may be difficult to chew and swallow. Among such foods are popcorn, peanut butter (particularly the crunchy variety), grapes, carrot circles, nuts, hot dogs (because of their casings), and raisins. Also, honey can cause infant botulism, a disease that may cause breathing difficulties and paralysis. Honey is not recommended for infants under a year old, but can safely be given to older children in moderation.

At all times when your child is eating, but especially when he or she has just started to eat finger foods, you'll want to watch carefully in case the child starts to choke. A large piece of cookie or cracker, a chunk of fruit or vegetable, or even a few crumbs can be enough to choke a child. See the photo and information on page 28 for the technique to use in the event your child chokes.

• Diarrhea and constipation. For diarrhea, your doctor may recommend what one pediatrician calls a BRATY diet (bananas, rice cereal, applesauce [without peels], toast, and yogurt) to firm up loose stools. Constipation generally isn't a problem for youngsters. Increased fluids and, depending on the child's ability to eat solids, high-fiber foods may help if stools are hard and difficult to pass. Breast-fed infants can continue to nurse.

• Fevers. When the baby's temperature rises above normal (98.6 degrees orally or about 99.6 rectally), you must compensate by increasing the amount of water he or she drinks. To prevent dehydration, infants with rectal temperatures of 104 degrees need almost 40 percent more water than they would normally require. Signs of dehydration include tearless crying and dry mouths and diapers. A properly hydrated child will urinate at least every four to six hours.

Any fever in a child under five months should be checked by a doctor. In older children, check with the doctor if the child's fever is above 101 degrees orally or 102 degrees rectally.

• Teething. Around the age of five to seven months, babies start to sprout teeth—usually the lower two front teeth first, followed by the upper two front teeth. When babies first begin to cut teeth, you may want to introduce finger foods such as zwieback toast, arrowroot biscuits, soft crackers, or special teething biscuits, which may ease any discomfort your baby has.

During the time the teeth are erupting, your baby may be a little irritable as a result of his or her swollen gums. The American Dental Association reminds parents that teething is a natural process. The baby's drooling and fussiness will disappear as soon as the emerging tooth breaks through the surface of the gums. In the meantime, to ease any discomfort, rub the baby's gums with a clean finger or with a small cool spoon. Special teething rings are available that can be placed in the refrigerator or freezer to cool before being given to the baby. In some extreme cases, medicines to numb the baby's gums may be prescribed.

• Vomiting. Nursing infants with illnesses that cause vomiting can continue to nurse; other similarly sick children should be encouraged to drink small amounts of clear liquids, including commercial products that help restore the chemical balance of the body's fluids. Always check with your baby's doctor if vomiting lasts through several feedings.

longer is interested in drinking the same amount of milk each day. That's normal as long as the baby thrives and grows.

Some parents take advantage of commercially prepared junior foods to bridge the gap between baby and adult foods. The almost limitless array of junior foods—including meat and vegetables, mixed cereals, starchy foods such as pasta and noodle dishes (starchy foods are recommended only for infants older than one year), and simple soups—is a boon to busy parents. The federal Food and Drug Administration cautions parents, however, that the sodium (salt) content of some of these foods may be high in relation to the recommended total daily levels of sodium for young children.

The FDA warns, too, that parents should read labels carefully before serving finger foods such as biscuits and meat sticks. To prevent choking, feed finger foods to babies only when they're in an upright position. As with all foods, these finger foods shouldn't be allowed in mouths of youngsters engaged in vigorous activities.

GUESS WHO'S COMING TO DINNER

Now that your toddler can eat some of the same foods you can, drink his or her milk from a cup (and spill only a little), and join in your conversation (even if it's only a few babbled words and a giggle or two), you'll want to start including him or her in your regular mealtime group. Children this age make interesting company. They're usually cheerful, generally intrigued by what's going on around them, and always amusing. Well, almost always.

Most parents like to work toddlers into the family meal routine gradually. Feeding even a hungry one-year-old is an often slow, sometimes frustrating, and usually messy process. Your youngster's ability to eat like Mom and Dad may be growing, but it will still take repeated efforts and a lot of help from you to make sure all, or at least the majority, of the food gets in the mouth.

For a while at least, you may want to wait until baby is finished, or mostly finished, before seating the rest of the family for their meal.

The toddler then can sit, for the most part satisfied, in his or her high chair or feeding table munching on finger foods.

If you use a high chair, make sure it has a wide base to keep it from tipping over, a removable tray that's easy to clean, and a strong locking mechanism to keep the tray from coming loose when your toddler rocks against it or pounds on it with a plastic cup. The tray itself should be big enough to hold one or more baby dishes, a cup, eating utensils, and maybe a toy. The tray should have a lip around the outside edge to help keep spilled food off the floor. Make sure the high chair has a sturdy restraint system (crotch strap and belt) to prevent your youngster from sliding under the tray or climbing out when your back is turned. And, finally, if you buy a painted wooden chair, make sure the paint is lead-free.

BABY'S MENU

In spite of your and your baby's delight in the change to self-feeding, there are some things you'll have to continue to help your youngster eat. Among them are soups, fruits and vegetables cooked to a mushy consistency, and, in general, any food that doesn't hold together.

Because the grinding teeth don't appear until after baby's first birthday, you'll need to hold off on foods that require heavy chewing. Postpone serving raw carrots and some meats and fruits at least until the first molars arrive.

You'll notice that your child is quick to express his or her opinions about food. Expect to be confused. One day your child will decide he or she loves lamb, then the next time you serve it, absolutely refuse to eat it.

Even though this erratic behavior can be frustrating, it's perfectly normal. And rest assured that, if offered a variety of good foods, your baby probably will choose a balanced diet.

By the time a baby is 18 months old, his or her table fare should be virtually the same as yours. The arrival of as many as 16 teeth means that more adult foods can be chewed and swallowed properly. For instance, the typical 18-month-old's favorite food list might include:

chopped hamburger, bananas, jelly, lunch meats, mashed potatoes, chicken (diced or chopped), cottage cheese, meat loaf (lightly seasoned), plain cookies, puddings, scrambled eggs, applesauce, orange slices, fruits (cooked, canned, and fresh), macaroni and spaghetti, bread and crackers, chopped or mashed vegetables.

Avoid foods that can't be easily chewed or that might become lodged in the throat. This list includes peanuts (and chunky peanut butter), popcorn, chunks of raw fruit or vegetable, fruits that contain seeds or stones or that have thick skins (unless removed beforehand), whole-kernel corn, grapes, and encased meats like hot dogs or sausages (unless cut into very fine pieces).

By 18 months of age, your toddler is probably eating three major meals each day, with snacks (appropriate fruits, unsalted crackers) at midmorning and midafternoon. For the big meals, include one main, filling dish like cereal, eggs, potatoes, macaroni, or spaghetti, plus a fruit or vegetable. Meats and other high-protein foods may be offered once or twice a day according to your doctor's or pediatrician's recommendations.

MAKING MEALTIME A HAPPY TIME

From almost their very first bites, children have a way of turning mealtime into a battleground. For instance, you've fixed strained beets and your child suddenly decides that today he or she doesn't like beets. You're late for work and your toddler decides that this is just the morning for a relaxed breakfast full of "conversation" and bread sculpting. You've just waxed the floor and your baby discovers the joy of tossing a plate over the edge of the high chair.

Here's some good advice: Stay calm. Don't worry if your child doesn't seem to be hungry or getting enough food. Remember that infants and children, when left to their own devices, will usually eat more than enough food to sustain themselves. As long as your baby is growing, active, and healthy, you can be sure the amount of food he or she is eating is sufficient. Concentrate your efforts on the *quality* of mealtime, not the *quantity* of food your baby eats.

Here are some other tips:

• Introduce new foods at the beginning of a meal while the baby is hungry. (A *really* hungry baby, however, may reject new foods. If so, switch back to familiar foods until the baby's appetite is partly satisfied.)

• Try offering only a few spoonfuls of new food the first time you serve it. That way, if it doesn't happen to agree with your child, you won't turn the meal into a major battle. Remove the food and gradually reintroduce it with subsequent meals.

• If your baby doesn't like certain meats or vegetables, try mixing them with foods he or she does like. Spread the new food on bread to form a finger food, or alternate spoonfuls with foods your youngster does like.

• Let your child hold a cup or spoon while being fed. This helps occupy a baby who's more interested in the world than the food before him or her.

• The American Dietetic Association urges parents not to nag, bribe, or try to force a child to eat. When children begin to play with their food, become restless, or otherwise indicate they're finished eating, let them leave the table or remove the food from the table.

• The ADA reminds parents that children don't need specific foods, they need specific nutrients. So if your baby balks at eating sweet potatoes, try a wedge of cantaloupe. If one meat is rejected, try another and wait a few weeks. The key to good nutrition is variety.

• If your child gets "stuck" on one or two particular foods for a few days in a row, the ADA recommends going along—for a while. If a certain category of food is rejected for more than two weeks, ask your doctor or a registered dietitian for an opinion.

• Here are some other pointers from the ADA: When your child is old enough, enlist his or her help in shopping for foods; feature a colorful variety of foods at each meal; cut foods in interesting shapes and arrange them attractively on the child's plate; serve food warm, rather than hot; moisten dry foods; keep foods separate—the ADA says it's not unusual for children to prefer their spaghetti sauce on the side.

TOO FAT?
TOO THIN?

The American Academy of Pediatrics calls obesity the most important nutritional disorder in the United States today. But the Academy also says it is possible at an early age to identify children who will grow up to be overweight. Such children include those whose parents are obese, those who gain weight rapidly during infancy, and those whose mothers use food to control behavior. The Academy says that there are some reasonable (but as yet unproven) ways to prevent obesity in children, including breast-feeding instead of bottle-feeding, delaying solid foods, feeding only to satisfy hunger and not to pacify a child, encouraging physical exercise, and serving low-calorie foods (young infants, however, should not be given skim milk).

The Academy's *Pediatric Nutrition Handbook* quotes a prominent researcher, Dr. Hilde Bruch: "If a child is fed when hungry, played with when needing attention, and encouraged to be active when restless, he or she is not likely to grow up inhibited and passive, or overstuffed and helpless, unable to control eating because every discomfort is misinterpreted as need to eat."

One of the main culprits in obesity is not what we eat as the main course, but what we eat for dessert. In most American households, desserts consist of lots of empty calories which, while tasting good, end up, eventually, as excess baggage around our middles.

So if you're concerned about your child's weight, avoid, as much as possible, the temptation to serve sweets. Try serving fruits instead of cookies, ice cream, or a candy bar. Limit sweet desserts to special occasions.

Admittedly, there's some parental manipulation involved in such restrictions, but by starting such practices while your child is young, you'll assist him or her in developing healthy eating habits. And it's better to start young before children have a chance—at Grandma's or their best friend's house—to develop a taste for more traditional, and fattening, desserts.

Some studies have shown that in their zeal to prevent obesity, some parents go too far in the opposite direction and so severely restrict their youngster's caloric intake that serious medical problems occur. Diagnosing and treating such malnourished or underweight children requires the expertise of a doctor.

Check with your pediatrician if you are concerned that your child is either overweight or underweight.

KITCHEN SAFETY

Once your baby is able to crawl or toddle around the house, the kitchen becomes something more than a place to eat. In a youngster's eyes, a kitchen is a magical place full of wonderful smells, activities, hidden recesses that contain strange and delightfully noisy toys, doors that reveal pretty colored bottles, and drawers that open easily, close with a bang, and contain bright shiny objects Mom and Dad wield with finesse.

But what your youngster won't realize are the dangers in the kitchen: pans of boiling water easily tipped over with just the tug of a tiny hand, dangling tablecloths, sharp knives, poisonous chemicals under the sink, electrical cords that fit nicely in tiny mouths, and big feet that can trip over a little boy or girl playing hide-and-seek under the table.

You'll want your child to spend time with you in the kitchen, of course. Make it safe by locking up all poisonous substances, placing knives and sharp cooking utensils completely out of your toddler's reach, and teaching the meaning of a firmly spoken "No!" or "Hot!"

One pediatrician recommends getting down on your hands and knees and pretending you're the same age as your child. Crawl around your own kitchen, exploring all the possible nooks and crannies your child might get into. When you encounter dangerous objects or substances, remove them from your child's reach.

Remember that almost nothing is more fun for a toddler than a few plastic plates, bowls, and cups, a few wooden spoons, and a dish towel. Set aside one easy-to-open cupboard or drawer just for your child's amusement and keep it well stocked with appropriate kitchen utensils. Check with your local fire department, extension service, or hospital for tips on childproofing your kitchen and house.

Eating out in restaurants need not be a hassle for you and your child. Make sure you select places that cater to children, with child-size portions, high chairs, speedy service, and foods your child especially enjoys.

EATING OUT

A child's ability to feed himself or herself table foods makes it both easier and more complicated when dining out. On the one hand, many restaurants provide high chairs and special children's menus. On the other hand, when your child is placed in the high chair and—unlike home—must wait for food to be served, he or she may raise a ruckus. You can avoid most of the commotion by bringing along some favorite finger foods, fruit, or small toys to keep your toddler occupied until his or her food is delivered.

Your youngster will, no doubt, develop a taste for fast foods. Whether fast foods contribute to overall good nutrition depends on what's on the menu, what you select, and how much and often you eat fast foods.

To make fast foods fit into a well-balanced diet, substitute milk, pure fruit juice, or water for soft drinks and shakes. Share shakes or french fries with parents or siblings to reduce the total calorie intake. Remove part of a bun from a burger to reduce calories. Compensate for the limited variety of foods at fast-food restaurants by making sure beans, other green and yellow vegetables, fruits, and fiber-containing breads and cereals are eaten at home, at school, or in other restaurants.

TAKING CARE OF TEETH

Your baby's first visit to the dentist should occur at about two years of age. Your family dentist may suggest that you see a specialist in children's dentistry, a pedodontist. But even before you take your child to the dentist for the first time, you can help him or her maintain good dental hygiene by buying a toothbrush and letting him or her mimic your daily brushing routine. You'll more than likely, though, have to finish up the cleaning after your child has had fun with the brush and toothpaste.

If the water your child drinks is not treated with fluoride, ask your dentist about supplemental fluoride treatments to prevent cavities. In any event, to prevent children under age five from ingesting too much fluoride contained in the toothpaste, parents should always keep watch while their youngsters are brushing their teeth.

Prevention is the most important part of good dental care, so you'll want to restrict sweets consumption and promote toothbrushing after every meal, more often if between-meal snacks contain sugar.

FOOD FOR THE REST OF THEIR LIVES

While your child may be extremely proficient when it comes to feeding himself or herself, you can't turn over all the responsibility for feeding to an 18-month-old. It's a good idea to continue to fill cups and glasses only partly full in anticipation of the sure-to-come spills. And while much of your child's diet at this age is the same as the rest of the family's, there are some things you must continue to help with.

You'll want to keep baby's food simple, saving the more sophisticatedly seasoned and presented fare until the child is a few years older. Simple foods—and combinations of simple foods—along with mild seasonings will make up the biggest portion of your child's diet for a few years yet.

Part and parcel of the stage of toddlerhood called the "terrible twos" is a picky appetite. It's part of this age for two reasons: the child needs less food because his or her rate of growth is slowing, and baby fat is being used up. Don't let this fool you into thinking your child isn't getting enough to eat. It's fine to let the child decide how much is enough as long as you've made sure that a variety of foods from the basic four food groups is available to choose from.

Indeed, making the transition from being the sole decision maker about your child's food to being a helpful bystander ready to provide direction is good training for the parenting that lies ahead. Just as you lose the ability to choose your child's food, so, too, will you lose the ability to make all kinds of other decisions for your child.

In matters of nutrition and general parenting alike, it's best to set out the options and step aside while your child makes the choice. The good nutritional foundation you've laid up to this point should help ensure that your child continues to eat well throughout a long and healthy life.

HEALTHY RECIPES AND SNACKS

Even though the American Council on Science and Health says commercially prepared baby foods can be "a wholesome addition to a child's diet," there's nothing quite like home cooking. Homemade foods allow you to take full advantage of the availability of fresh produce. And forgoing store-bought baby foods frees you to serve your young child some of the foods you serve the rest of the family. When preparing the same foods for your baby and your family, however, remember to remove the baby's portion before salting and seasoning. In addition, cook food for the baby till it's very tender so that it can be pureed to a smooth, lump-free texture.

Despite the many advantages of homemade foods, for convenience and variety, you may want to serve store-bought baby foods in addition to the ones you cook yourself. Remember, solid foods of any sort are not recommended for infants under four months of age. Homemade baby foods made with certain fresh vegetables, such as spinach, beets, and carrots, should not be fed to infants under four months because they may contain nitrates that—in sufficient quantities—may be harmful.

On the next three pages you'll find recipes for some of your baby's first solid foods. Following that are recipes just right for the growing child as well as the entire family. No matter what foods you serve your child, remember that there is another ingredient essential to every meal. That's the love only you as a concerned parent can add to the food you make for your child.

Use fresh ingredients and make sure your kitchen equipment and hands are clean.

Cook vegetables till very tender. Test for doneness by pressing with a fork.

Puree foods in a blender or food processor. Stop blender to scrape sides as needed.

Spoon pureed foods into ice-cube trays for freezing. Thaw cubes as needed.

MAKING BABY FOODS

Use these directions with baby-food recipes on the next two pages. Choose fresh ingredients; omit seasonings. Wash fruits and vegetables well.

Boiling vegetables: Prepare vegetables; add to medium saucepan with specified amount of boiling water. Return to boiling; reduce heat. Simmer, covered, for time indicated in recipe or till very tender. Drain. Depending on recipe, reserve cooking liquid to use when processing.

Steaming vegetables: Prepare vegetables. Place steamer basket in saucepan. Add water to just below bottom of steamer basket; bring to boiling. Add vegetables. Steam, covered, for the time indicated in recipe or till very tender. Use cooking liquid when processing.

Pureeing baby foods: Place prepared foods in a blender container or food processor bowl. Cover; blend or process till pureed, adding liquid to make desired consistency. Vary the degree of processing according to the baby's needs: process till very smooth for baby's first foods, leave a little texture for junior foods.

Freezing/thawing/heating: Spoon pureed food into ice-cube trays. Cover; freeze till firm. When frozen, remove cubes; place in freezer bag. Seal, label, and freeze up to several weeks. To thaw, place a serving in refrigerator 5 to 6 hours or overnight. Or, place 1 portion (3 to 4 frozen cubes) in small dish; set in pan of warm water 20 minutes to thaw (change water once or twice). To heat, place 1 portion in a saucepan over low heat 10 to 12 minutes, stirring often. Or, thaw and heat as follows: place 1 portion in a microwave-safe dish; micro-cook on 100% power (high) 1 to 1½ minutes, stirring once.

COOKED FRUIT

Boiling: Wash, peel, core, and cut up 1 pound *apples or ripe pears*. (Apple choices include Jonathan, Wealthy, Winesap, and Red Delicious.) *Or,* wash, peel, remove pits from, and cut up 1 pound *ripe peaches or nectarines*.

In a medium saucepan combine desired fruit and 2 tablespoons *water*. Bring to boiling. Reduce heat. Cover and simmer till fruit is very tender, stirring once. Allow about 10 minutes for apples, 12 to 14 minutes for pears, and 8 to 10 minutes for peaches and nectarines. *Do not drain the fruit.*

Place fruit and liquid in a blender container or food processor bowl. Cover. Blend or process till the mixture is very smooth, adding 1 to 2 tablespoons *apple juice or water* as necessary to make desired consistency. Cool. Serve or freeze (see directions, *opposite*). Makes about 1½ cups.

Micro-cooking: Prepare desired fruit as above. In a 1½-quart microwave-safe casserole combine fruit and the water. Micro-cook, covered, on 100% power (high) till fruit is very tender, stirring once. Allow 3 to 4 minutes for apples, 5 to 7 minutes for pears, peaches, and nectarines. *Do not drain.* Puree as above, adding *apple juice or water* as necessary to make desired consistency.

FRESH FRUIT

Wash, peel, core, and cut up 1 small *apple or* half of a small *ripe pear*. Or, wash, peel, remove pit from, and cut up 1 small *ripe peach or nectarine*. Place fruit in a blender container or food processor bowl. Cover. Blend or process till fruit is very smooth, adding a little *apple juice or water* if necessary (1 to 3 tablespoons depending on fruit) till fruit is pureed. Serve the fruit immediately.

For bananas, peel half of a very *ripe banana*. Place banana in a bowl and mash till very smooth using a fork. Serve the mashed banana immediately.

GREEN BEANS

Boiling: Wash 1 pound *green beans;* cut beans into 1-inch pieces. Add beans to a medium saucepan with ¾ cup *boiling unsalted water*. Return to boiling; reduce heat. Simmer, covered, for 20 to 25 minutes or till beans are very tender. Drain, reserving liquid. Puree beans, adding 1 to 2 tablespoons cooking liquid to make desired consistency. Cool. Serve or freeze (see directions, *opposite*). Makes about 1⅓ cups.

Steaming: Prepare *green beans* as above. Steam, covered, for 25 to 30 minutes or till very tender (see directions, *opposite*). Puree the beans, adding 1 to 2 tablespoons cooking liquid.

BEETS

Boiling: Scrub 1 pound *beets*. Cut off all but 1 inch of tops and roots. Add beets to a medium saucepan with 1 inch *boiling unsalted water*. Return to boiling; reduce heat. Simmer, covered, about 40 minutes or till beets are very tender. Drain. When beets are cool enough to handle, slip off skins. Cut up beets. Puree, adding ⅓ to ½ cup *water* to make desired consistency. Cool. Serve or freeze (see directions, *opposite*). Makes 1½ cups.

Steaming: Prepare *beets* as above. Steam, covered, for 45 to 50 minutes or till very tender (see directions, *opposite*). Peel and cut up. Puree, adding *water*.

CARROTS

Boiling: Scrub 1 pound *carrots*. Slice carrots. Add carrots to a medium saucepan with ⅔ cup *boiling unsalted water*. Return to boiling; reduce heat. Simmer, covered, about 25 minutes or till carrots are very tender. Drain, reserving liquid. Puree, adding about 1 tablespoon cooking liquid to make desired consistency. Cool. Serve or freeze (see directions, *opposite*). Makes about 1¼ cups.

Steaming: Prepare *carrots* as above. Steam, covered, about 35 minutes or till very tender (see directions, *opposite*). Puree, adding ⅓ to ½ cup cooking liquid.

PEAS

Boiling: Add one 10-ounce package frozen *peas* (2 cups) to saucepan with ½ cup *boiling unsalted water.* Return to boiling; reduce heat. Simmer, covered, for 10 to 15 minutes or till peas are very tender. Drain, reserving liquid. Puree, adding ⅓ to ½ cup cooking liquid to make desired consistency. Cool. Serve or freeze (see directions, page 40). Makes 1¼ cups.

Steaming: Steam frozen *peas,* covered, for 15 to 18 minutes or till very tender (see directions, page 40). Puree, adding ⅓ to ½ cup cooking liquid to make desired consistency.

SPINACH

Boiling: Wash ½ pound *spinach* and remove stems. Tear spinach and add to a medium saucepan with 2 tablespoons *water.* Cover and cook for 3 to 5 minutes. Drain, reserving liquid. Puree, adding 1 to 2 tablespoons cooking liquid to make desired consistency. Cool. Serve or freeze (see directions, page 40). Makes ⅔ cup.

Steaming: Prepare *spinach* as above. Steam, covered, for 3 to 5 minutes (see directions, page 40). Puree, adding 1 to 2 tablespoons cooking liquid to make desired consistency.

Micro-cooking: Prepare *spinach* as above. Place spinach in a 2-quart microwave-safe casserole. Add 1 tablespoon *water.* Micro-cook, covered, on 100% power (high) for 3 to 5 minutes. Drain spinach, reserving liquid. Puree, adding about 1 tablespoon cooking liquid to make desired consistency.

SWEET POTATOES

Boiling: Scrub 2 medium *sweet potatoes* (6 to 8 ounces each). Cut off woody portions and ends of potatoes. Cook, covered, in enough *boiling unsalted water* to cover for 25 to 35 minutes or till potatoes are very tender. Drain, discarding cooking water. When cool enough to handle, peel and cut up potatoes. Puree, adding ½ to ⅔ cup *water* to make desired consistency. Cool. Serve or freeze (see directions, page 40). Makes about 1¼ cups.

Micro-cooking: Scrub 2 medium *sweet potatoes* (6 to 8 ounces each). Cut off woody portions and ends. Prick skins in several places. Arrange potatoes on a microwave-safe plate. Micro-cook, uncovered, on 100% power (high) for 8 to 10 minutes or till potatoes are tender, rearranging once. When cool enough to handle, scrape potato from peels. Puree, adding ¾ to 1 cup *water* to make desired consistency.

MEAT

Select lean boneless *beef round steak or chicken pieces.* Trim fat (remove skin from chicken, if desired). Cut beef into cubes.

In a saucepan add 1 cup *water* for each cup (8 ounces) beef. *Or,* cover chicken with *water.* Bring to boiling; reduce heat. Simmer, covered, till meat is tender. Allow 1 hour for beef and 1¼ hours for chicken pieces.

Drain meat, reserving liquid. Skim off fat if necessary. Measure meat, cutting chicken from bones to measure.

In a blender container or food processor bowl place ½ cup cooking liquid for each 1 cup cooked meat. Add the meat to the cooking liquid. Cover and blend or process till meat is pureed, adding more liquid if necessary, and stopping to scrape sides. Cool. Serve or freeze (see directions, page 40). Makes about 1 cup puree for each cup of uncooked meat.

Ground meat: Cook 1 pound lean *ground meat* till no pink remains. In a blender container or food processor bowl place ½ cup *milk or water.* Add the cooked meat with juices. Cover and puree, stopping often to scrape sides. If necessary, add 2 to 4 tablespoons additional liquid to make desired consistency. Cool. Serve or freeze (see directions, page 40). Makes 1½ cups puree.

SCRAMBLED EGGS

6 eggs
⅓ cup milk *or* light cream
¼ teaspoon salt
Dash pepper
1 tablespoon margarine *or* butter

In a bowl beat together eggs, milk or cream, salt, and pepper. Stir with a fork to mix.

In a 10-inch skillet melt margarine or butter over medium heat. Pour in the egg mixture. Cook, without stirring, till mixture begins to set on the bottom and around the edges. Using a large spoon or spatula, lift and fold partially cooked eggs so uncooked portion flows underneath. Continue cooking over medium heat for 2 to 3 minutes or till eggs are cooked throughout but are still glossy and moist. Remove from heat immediately. Makes 3 servings.

Microwave directions: In a microwave-safe 1½-quart casserole melt the margarine or butter on 100% power (high) for 30 to 40 seconds. In a bowl beat together eggs, milk or cream, salt, and pepper. Pour egg mixture into casserole with margarine. Micro-cook, uncovered, on high for 4 to 5 minutes or till eggs are almost set, pushing cooked portions to the center every 30 to 60 seconds as needed. Let eggs stand about 1 minute or till set.

GARDEN-PATCH MACARONI

1 cup mixed spinach and carrot corkscrew *or* elbow macaroni
2 tablespoons margarine *or* butter
2 tablespoons all-purpose flour
Dash pepper
1 cup milk
1 cup cubed American cheese (4 ounces)
1 cup loose-pack frozen peas *or* cut green beans

Cook the corkscrew or elbow macaroni according to package directions. Drain macaroni and set aside.

Meanwhile, for sauce, in a medium saucepan melt margarine or butter. Stir in flour and pepper; add milk all at once. Cook and stir till mixture is thickened and bubbly. Add cheese and stir till cheese melts.

Stir together cooked macaroni, sauce, and frozen vegetables. Transfer mixture to a 1-quart casserole. Bake, uncovered, in a 350° oven for 20 to 25 minutes or till mixture is heated through. If desired, slice 1 medium *tomato* and arrange the slices on top of casserole; bake about 5 minutes more or till tomato is warm. Makes 4 servings.

CHOW-TIME CHICKEN CHOWDER

2 cups chicken broth
1 cup loose-pack frozen cut broccoli
1 medium carrot, shredded (½ cup)
¼ cup quick-cooking brown rice
1 tablespoon dried minced onion
Dash pepper
1 cup milk
1 tablespoon all-purpose flour
1½ cups cubed cooked chicken (8 ounces)

In a large saucepan stir together chicken broth, frozen broccoli, shredded carrot, *uncooked* rice, onion, and pepper. Bring the mixture to boiling. Reduce the heat. Cover and simmer the mixture for 12 to 15 minutes or till vegetables and rice are tender.

Stir together milk and flour. Stir into broth mixture in saucepan. Cook and stir over medium heat till the mixture is thickened and bubbly. Cook and stir for 1 minute more. Stir in chicken. Cook about 3 minutes longer or till heated through. Makes 4 servings.

ALPHABET CAKES

- ¾ cup whole wheat flour
- ½ cup all-purpose flour
- 2 tablespoons brown sugar
- 1 teaspoon baking powder
- ¼ teaspoon baking soda
- 1 beaten egg
- 1½ cups buttermilk
- 1 tablespoon cooking oil
  Pancake and waffle syrup

In a medium mixing bowl stir together whole wheat flour, all-purpose flour, sugar, baking powder, and baking soda. Combine egg, buttermilk, and oil. Add all at once to the flour mixture. Stir till combined but still slightly lumpy.

For each pancake, carefully spoon ¼ cup to ½ cup batter onto a hot, lightly greased griddle or heavy skillet to form a letter or shape (for example, initials, bunny, bear, turtle, car, cat, funny face, snowman, flower, or star).

Cook till golden brown, turning when pancakes have bubbly surfaces and slightly dry edges. Serve with pancake and waffle syrup. Makes about nine 4-inch pancakes.

FRENCH TOAST

- 4 slices bread
- 2 beaten eggs
- ½ cup milk
- ¼ teaspoon vanilla
- ⅛ teaspoon ground cinnamon
  Margarine *or* butter
  Sweetened fruit, powdered sugar, *or*
  maple-flavored syrup

If desired, for firmer toast, put bread on a rack. Cover with paper towels and leave overnight to dry slightly. In a shallow bowl beat together eggs, milk, vanilla, and cinnamon. Dip bread into egg mixture; coat both sides. In a 12-inch skillet cook bread on both sides in a small amount of hot margarine or butter over medium-high heat till golden; add margarine as needed. Serve with fruit, sugar, or syrup. Makes 4 slices.

NESTED EGGS

- 2 large potatoes
- ¼ cup milk
- ½ cup shredded cheddar cheese
  (2 ounces)
- ¼ cup shredded carrot
- ¼ cup shredded zucchini
- ¼ teaspoon salt
- ⅛ teaspoon pepper
- 4 eggs

Peel and quarter potatoes. Cook potatoes, covered, in boiling water for 20 to 25 minutes or till tender. Drain. Mash with a potato masher or on low speed of an electric mixer. Add milk to mashed potatoes and mash till combined. Stir in cheese, carrot, zucchini, salt, and pepper.

Spoon potato mixture into 4 lightly greased 10-ounce casseroles. With the back of a spoon, push potato mixture from centers, building up sides. Carefully break *one* egg into the center of *each* casserole. Place casseroles on a baking sheet. Bake in a 425° oven about 15 minutes or till eggs are desired doneness. Makes 4 servings.

PUSH-BUTTON PEACH SHAKES

- 1 cup frozen unsweetened peach
  slices, *or* one 8¾-ounce can
  peach slices, chilled and drained
- ½ of an 8-ounce carton (½ cup)
  vanilla yogurt
- ¼ cup milk
- 1 tablespoon sugar

In a blender container combine the peach slices, vanilla yogurt, milk, and sugar*. Cover the blender container and blend till the mixture is smooth. Pour into 2 small glasses. Makes 2 (4-ounce) servings.

*If using canned peaches, omit the sugar.

PUDDING POWER

- ¼ **cup sugar**
- 2 **teaspoons cornstarch**
- 1 **12-ounce can evaporated skim milk**
- 1 **beaten egg**
- 1 **tablespoon margarine *or* butter**
- 2 **teaspoons vanilla**
- ¼ **cup chopped fresh *or* dried fruit,**
   ***or* 2 tablespoons miniature**
   semisweet chocolate pieces

In a medium saucepan stir together sugar and cornstarch. Stir in milk. Cook and stir over medium heat till thickened and bubbly. Cook and stir for 2 minutes more. Remove from heat.

Gradually stir about *1 cup* of the hot mixture into egg. Return all to mixture in saucepan. Cook and stir over low heat for 2 minutes more. *Do not boil.* Remove from heat. Stir in margarine or butter and vanilla till margarine or butter melts.

Stir in fruit or chocolate. (If adding chocolate pieces, allow pudding to cool for 20 minutes, then gently stir in chocolate pieces just till distributed.) Pour into a bowl. Cover surface with clear plastic wrap. Chill without stirring. Makes 4 servings.

Chocolate Pudding Power: Prepare Pudding Power as above, *except* increase sugar to ⅓ cup, add 2 tablespoons *unsweetened cocoa powder* to the sugar mixture, and increase margarine or butter to 2 tablespoons.

Butterscotch Pudding Power: Prepare Pudding Power as above, *except* substitute ¼ cup packed *brown sugar* for sugar and increase margarine or butter to 2 tablespoons.

SHAKY SHAPES

- 1½ **cups water**
- 3 **envelopes unflavored gelatin**
- 1 **6-ounce can frozen apple, cranberry, orange, tangerine, *or* grape juice concentrate**

Pour the water into a medium saucepan. Sprinkle unflavored gelatin over water and let stand 1 minute to soften. Bring mixture to boiling, stirring constantly till gelatin dissolves. Remove the mixture from heat.

Stir desired frozen juice concentrate into gelatin mixture in saucepan. Stir till juice concentrate melts. Pour mixture into a foil-lined 8x8x2-inch pan. Cover and chill in the refrigerator till the gelatin mixture is firm.

Invert the gelatin mixture onto a cutting board. Remove the foil. Use cookie cutters or a table knife to cut the gelatin into shapes. Makes about 36 (1½-inch) pieces.

CRITTER CRACKERS

- ¾ **cup whole wheat flour**
- ¼ **cup cornmeal**
- ¼ **cup grated Parmesan cheese**
- 1 **teaspoon baking powder**
- ¼ **teaspoon salt**
- ¼ **cup margarine *or* butter**
- ¼ **cup milk *or* plain yogurt**

In a medium mixing bowl stir together flour, cornmeal, grated Parmesan cheese, baking powder, and salt. Then cut in margarine or butter till the mixture resembles fine crumbs. Stir in milk or plain yogurt to make a stiff dough.

On a lightly floured surface roll the dough to ⅛-inch thickness. Cut with cookie cutters or a sharp knife into animal or other shapes. Place the cutouts on a greased baking sheet. Prick the surfaces of the cutouts with the tines of a fork, if desired.

Bake in a 375° oven for 4 to 6 minutes or till crackers are brown on the bottom. Turn crackers over with a spatula. Bake for 3 to 5 minutes more or till brown on the bottom. (For large crackers, you may need to bake longer on each side.) Cool crackers on a wire rack. Makes 48 (2-inch) crackers.

HEIGHT & WEIGHT
BIRTH TO ONE YEAR

These charts show how quickly babies grow in their first year of life. But keep in mind that each baby's progress is unique. Use the charts as general guides and don't be concerned if your child is a little ahead of or behind the averages.

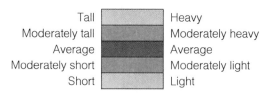

Tall — Heavy
Moderately tall — Moderately heavy
Average — Average
Moderately short — Moderately light
Short — Light

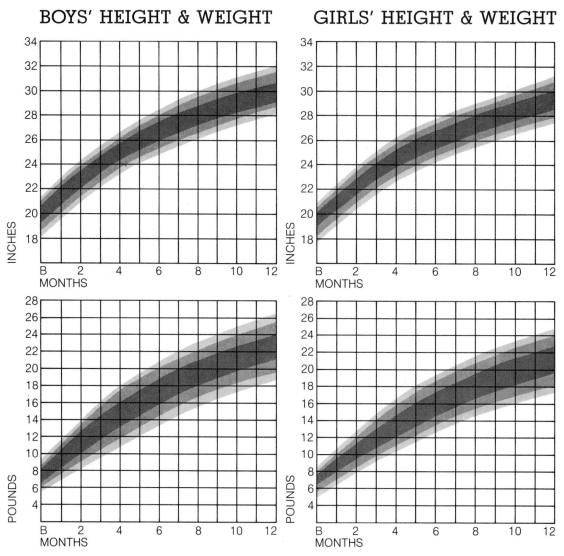

BOYS' HEIGHT & WEIGHT

GIRLS' HEIGHT & WEIGHT

ONE THROUGH SIX YEARS

After his or her first birthday, your baby's growth rate will slow. Although these charts don't show it, growth usually occurs in spurts and bursts, which are a normal part of every child's development.

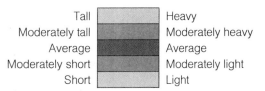

Tall	Heavy
Moderately tall	Moderately heavy
Average	Average
Moderately short	Moderately light
Short	Light

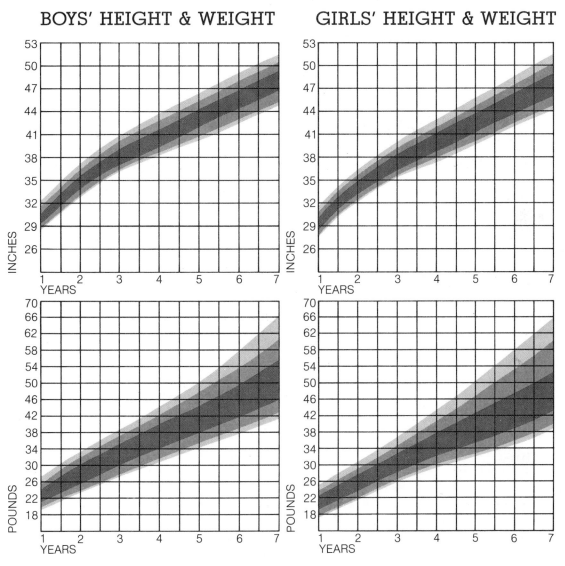

BOYS' HEIGHT & WEIGHT

GIRLS' HEIGHT & WEIGHT